Feel the Power

Energy All Around

by Rebecca Weber

Content and Reading Adviser: Mary Beth Fletcher, Ed.D.
Educational Consultant/Reading Specialist
The Carroll School, Lincoln, Massachusetts

Compass Point Books ✦ Minneapolis, Minnesota

Compass Point Books
3109 West 50th Street, #115
Minneapolis, MN 55410

Visit Compass Point Books on the Internet at *www.compasspointbooks.com*
or e-mail your request to *custserv@compasspointbooks.com*

Photographs ©: TRIP/S. Grant, cover; TRIP/B. Turner, 4; Comstock, Inc., 5; Imagestate, 6, 8;
PhotoDisc, 7, 9, 17; TRIP/M. Thornton, 10; TRIP, 11, 13, 15; TRIP/H. Rogers, 12, 16;
Adam Woolfitt/Corbis, 14; EyeWire/Getty Images, 19; Two Coyotes Studio/Mary Foley, 20, 21.

Project Manager: Rebecca Weber McEwen
Editor: Heidi Schoof
Photo Selectors: Rebecca Weber McEwen and Heidi Schoof
Designers: Les Tranby and Jaime Martens

Library of Congress Cataloging-in-Publication Data

Weber, Rebecca.
  Feel the power: energy all around / by Rebecca Weber.
     p. cm. — (Spyglass books)
Summary: Provides a brief introduction to various forms of energy,
including sun, wind, water, and people power.
  ISBN 978-0-7565-0386-4 (hardcover)
  ISBN 978-0-7565-1048-0 (paperback)
  1. Power resources—Juvenile literature. [1. Power resources.]
  I. Title. II. Series.
  TJ163.23 .W43 2002
  621.042—dc21
                              2002002755

Contents

Sun Power

Long ago, people learned that the sun was powerful. They built their homes so the sun could keep them warm in the winter.

Sun dial

Today, people still use the sun's power. They collect and store *energy* from the sun. It can warm a house. It can run a car.

Solar-powered car

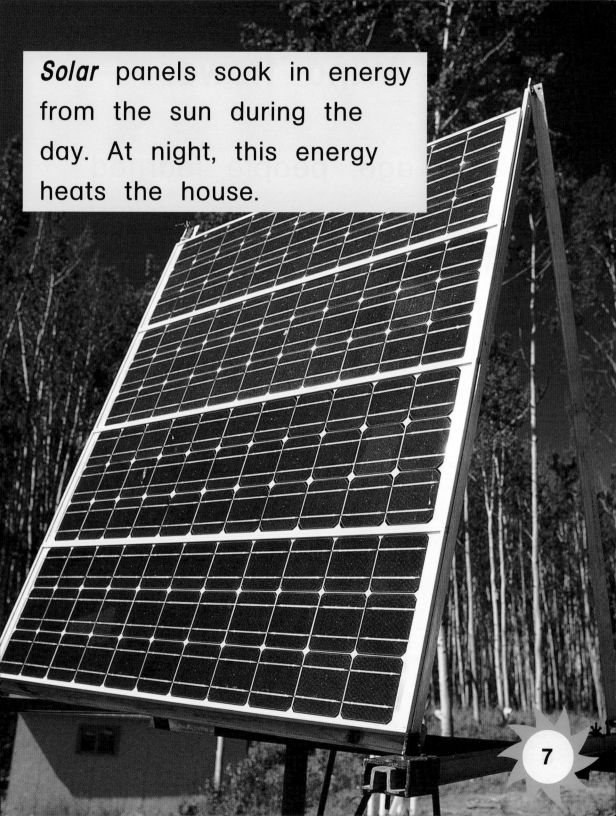

Solar panels soak in energy from the sun during the day. At night, this energy heats the house.

Wind Power

Long ago, people learned that the wind was powerful. Wind turned a windmill to pump water out of a well. Wind pushed sails to move boats across the water.

Windmill

9

Today, people still use the wind's power. When wind turns these windmills, it makes *electricity* for people's homes. Wind lets people fly a kite.

Windmills

11

Water Power

Long ago, people learned that water was powerful. People traveled along rivers. Rushing water turned water wheels, which then moved stones to grind corn.

Water wheel

Riverboat

13

Today, people still use the water's power. Water moving through a *dam* makes electricity for many homes. Water flows through a dry field to keep plants alive.

Dam

People Power

Long ago, people learned that their brains were powerful, too. They thought up new *inventions.* They used tools to build amazing things.

People set up
these heavy stones
using simple tools.

Today, people still use brain power. When you solve a math problem, you are being powerful, too!

Make a Solar Panel

You will need:

- a bright, sunny window

- a black plate, or
  a black piece of cloth

Put the black plate in a sunny place next to the window.

Let it stay there ten minutes.

Take the plate back to your desk.

Feel the plate. It is giving off solar energy.

Glossary

dam–something that stops water from flowing, causing it to back up and make a pool

electricity–a kind of energy that helps make things work, such as lightbulbs

energy–power that can be used

invention–a tool or machine that does something in a new way

solar–when something gets energy from the sun

sun dial–a tool that tells the time when the sun casts a shadow on it

Learn More

Books

Arnold, Guy. *Water, Wind, and Solar Power.* Illustrated by Peter Harper. New York: Franklin Watts, 1990.

Dineen, Jacqueline. *Oil, Gas, and Coal.* Austin, Tex.: Raintree Steck-Vaughn Publishers, 1995.

Lowery, Linda. *Earth Day.* Minneapolis, Minn.: Carolrhoda Books, 1991.

On the Web

For more information on this topic, use FactHound.

1. Go to *www.facthound.com*
2. Type in this book ID: 0756503868
3. Click on the *Fetch It* button.

FactHound will find the best Web sites for you.

Index

GR: H
Word Count: 191

From Rebecca Weber

I grew up in the country, so I
have always loved nature. I enjoy
teaching people about the world
and how to take care of it.

24